Fruit Salad

What's long, orange and wears diapers?

Why do people put stakes by a tomato plant?

Can an orange box?

A baby carrot.

To make the tomato catch up.

No, but the tomato can.

What's yellow and hides in a cave?

What's green and sings?

A banana that owes money.

Elvis Parsley.

What's red and goes, "Putt, putt, putt?"

Did Eve ever have a date with Adam?

An outboard apple.

No, it was an apple.

The Funny Farm

What do you call a sleeping bull?

A bulldozer.

Why did Santa Claus grow a garden?

What goes, "Oom, oom?"

So he could ho, ho, ho.

A cow walking backwards.

What did the mother goat say to her son?

Where does a sheep get his hair cut?

Why do cows wear cowbells?

"Stop butting in when I'm talking."

At a baa-baa shop.

Because their horns don't work.

History's Mysteries

Why does the Statue of Liberty stand in New York Harbor?

When did they first say, "God Bless America?"

What's worse than singing the Star Spangled Banner for hours?

19

Because it can't sit down.

When it sneezed.

Singing the Stars and Stripes Forever.

Why did Betsy Ross go to the doctor?

What did they call the Englishman who built the British navy?

What did George Washington say to his father when he chopped down the cherry tree?

She started seeing stars and stripes.

Sir Launchalot.

"Pop-eye did it."

Here Come the Elephants

Why is an elephant big, gray, and wrinkled?

What's gray and blue?

Because if it were little, round and white you'd think it was an aspirin.

An elephant holding his breath.

How can you tell there's an elephant under your bed?

What's big and green and has a trunk?

Why do elephants wear ripple-soled shoes?

You'll be close to the ceiling.

An unripe elephant.

To give the ants a fifty-fifty chance.

What's gray and has purple feet?

An elephant that makes his own wine.

What Did He Say?

What did the boy octopus say to his girl friend?

"Let's walk hand in hand, in hand, in hand, in hand."

What did the baby corn say to the mother corn?

What did the necktie say to the hat?

What did the South Pole say to the North Pole?

31

"Where's pop corn?"

"You go on ahead; I'll hand around."

"Hi, you all."

What did the big chimney say to the little chimney?

What did the jack say to the car?

33

"You're too young to smoke."

"Can I give you a lift?"

Birds and the Bees

What did the papa lightning bug say to the mama lightning bug?

What do you call a crazy blackbird?

"Isn't Junior bright for his age?"

A raven maniac.

Why does a stork stand on one foot?

What did the flower say to the bee?

Why is the sky so high?

If he'd lift the other foot, he'd fall down.

"Quit bugging me!"

So the birds won't bump their heads.

In a Pickle

What is a pickle?

What's green and pecks on trees?

A cucumber with a sour disposition.

Woody Woodpickle.

What's green and jumps ten feet?

What's green and goes, "Tooty, toot, toot?"

What's green and says, "Oink, oink, oink?"

A pickle with hiccups.

A pickle-o.

Porky the Pickle.

42

Who grows cucumbers for a pickle factory?

What's green, bumpy and flies?

The farmer in the dill.

Super Pickle.

Animal Crackers

What did the monkey say when he rode down the giraffe's neck?

What has antlers and squeaks?

So long.

Mickey Moose.

You Tell 'Em

You tell 'em balloon. You're on the up and up.

You tell 'em cabbage. You've got the head.

You tell 'em salad. I'm dressing.

You tell 'em lamp. I'm in the dark.

You tell 'em clock. You've got the time.

You tell 'em June. And don't July.

You tell 'em operator. You've got their number.

You tell 'em pony. I'm a little horse.

Books You'll Never Read

I Hate Homework by I.M. Laizee

How to Fix a Television Set by Yul B. Sorry

I'm Tired by Anita Rest

Birds by C. Gull

How to Deal with Mistakes by E. Ray Sur

How to Write a Letter by Adeline Moore

Red Vegetables by Tom A. Toe

The Monster by Frank N. Stein

Cats by Ann Gora

As Funny As

That joke was as funny as a flood in an Alka-Seltzer factory.

That joke was as funny as a submarine with a screen door.

That joke was as funny as a rubber crutch.

That joke was as funny as a raincheck in the Houston Astrodome.

That joke was as funny as an igloo with central heating.

Suggestions for Further Reading

Adler, Bill. *World's Worst Riddles and Jokes.* Grosset and Dunlop, 1976.

Cole, William. *Book of Giggles.* Collins-World, 1970.

Emrich, Duncan. *The Whim-Wham Book.* Four Winds, 1975.

Fox, Sonny. *Funnier Than the First One.* Putnam, 1972.

Hoke, Helen. *Jokes, Giggles and Guffaws.* Franklin Watts, 1975.

Morrison, Lillian. *Best Wishes, Amen.* T. Y. Crowell, 1974.

Schwartz, Alvin. *Tomfoolery.* Lippincott, 1973.

Thorndike, Susan. *The Electric Radish and Other Jokes.* Doubleday, 1973.

Wiesner, William. *How Silly Can You Be?* Seabury, 1975.